EASY PHP - Handy Guide

Discover the World of Web Programming

INDEX

Intro	4

Development environment

❖ Introduction — 5
❖ Configuration — 5

Basics

❖ PHP & HTML — 6
❖ Opening and closing tags — 6
❖ Data types — 7
❖ Comments — 7
❖ Variables — 8
❖ Echo function — 9
❖ Error displays — 10
❖ Constants — 11
❖ Expressions — 12
❖ Operators — 13

Control structures and cycles

❖ If, else — 17
❖ Switch statement — 17
❖ Ternary operator — 18
❖ For, while and do — 19
❖ Break and continue — 20

Texts and strings

❖ PHP functions for string manipulation — 22
❖ String formatting — 23
❖ String comparison — 25
❖ Date and time — 28
❖ Regular expressions — 29

Array

❖	Arrays	31
❖	Associative arrays	32
❖	Functions dedicated to arrays	33
❖	Array cycles	34
❖	Multidimensional arrays	35
❖	Data validation	36

Functions

❖	Functions	38
❖	Recursive functions	39
❖	Visibility of variables	40
❖	Pass by value or by reference	41

PHP methods

❖	HTTP requests	43
❖	GET and POST	43
❖	Manage Cookies	44
❖	Manage sessions	45
❖	REQUEST and SERVER	46

Object Oriented Programming (OOP)

❖	Introduction	48
❖	Classes and objects	48
❖	Builder and destroyer	49
❖	Inheritance	50
❖	Visibility of properties and methods	52
❖	Polymorphism	53
❖	Static methods and properties	54

Plus

❖	Include and require	56
❖	Send an email	57
❖	Interact with MySql Databases	57

❖ Manipulate JSON   59

❖ Manage files   60

❖ Password management   61

Outro   63

Intro

Welcome to **EASY PHP**, a comprehensive guide designed to give you the essentials to start programming using the powerful PHP language. This manual will take you into the world of web development, providing you with the basics needed to create dynamic and interactive applications.

PHP, short for "PHP: Hypertext Preprocessor", is a scripting language widely used for developing web applications. Thanks to its intuitive syntax and the flexibility it offers, PHP has become a favorite tool for developers to create dynamic web pages and manage data from databases.

This book was designed for anyone new to PHP. Regardless of your level of programming experience, you'll learn the fundamentals of PHP, from handling variables and operators to using loops and conditions to control program flow.

During the learning path, we'll also explore topics such as string handling, interacting with forms, using arrays to collect and manipulate data, and introducing the concepts of functions and libraries.

With the help of practical examples and clear explanations, you will be able to gradually develop your PHP programming skills. This manual will provide you with a solid foundation upon which you can build your future web applications and give you the confidence to explore more advanced concepts in the future.

Whether you're a computer science student, an aspiring web developer, or just curious about learning a new programming language, we'll take you on your PHP learning journey.

So, without further ado, get ready to immerse yourself in the fascinating world of PHP and discover the infinite possibilities that this language can offer!

Development environment

Introduction

This manual includes a dedicated development environment, which means it avoids the need to set up a local development environment, which can vary from computer to computer. Using the included development environment is more convenient and faster, as no software installation is required. Furthermore, it will be possible to test written pages directly from the browser.

Configuration

To access the dedicated development environment, connect to the site https://easy-php.cloud/board .
After registering or logging in, you will immediately find the work environment ready for use.

To create a new page click on the 'add' button, in the left side column. Enter a name for the page respecting the constraints and press 'Create'. You will find the summary of all the pages you have created in the left side column.

To write on a page, click on its name: the text editor will open, allowing you to write code on it.

Using the 'open in browser' button, at the top right of the text editor, you can open the page in the browser, thus executing the code you wrote. Always remember to save the changes using the 'Save' button, at the bottom right, before opening a page in the browser, otherwise the code just written will not be executed but the previous one.

You can delete a page using the button at the top right of the text editor, showing the figure of the trash can.

Basics

PHP & HTML

PHP and HTML are two complementary technologies that are often used together in web development. Each of them plays a specific role in the process of creating dynamic and interactive web pages.

HTML (Hypertext Markup Language) is the standard markup language for creating and structuring web pages. HTML defines the elements and tags that are used to organize the content of a page, such as headings, paragraphs, tables, images, links and many more. HTML provides a basic framework for the layout and appearance of a web page.

PHP, on the other hand, is a server-side scripting language. This means that the PHP code is executed on the web server before the page is sent to the user's browser. PHP allows you to create dynamic web pages, where content can be generated based on conditions, input data or user interactions. With PHP, you can connect to a database to retrieve or store information, perform calculations, manage user sessions, and more.

The combination of PHP and HTML is powerful because it allows programming logic and data manipulation to be embedded within HTML pages. It is common to see blocks of PHP code embedded within an HTML document, usually within special tags called "PHP tags" or "PHP delimiter tags" (e.g.<?php ... ?>). These tags tell the web server that the code contained within them should be interpreted as PHP and not HTML.

Using PHP and HTML together, it is possible to create dynamic pages that adapt to user needs and available data. For example, you can create a registration form that sends the data entered by the user to a PHP file for processing and subsequent saving in the database. In this way, it is possible to create interactive and customized websites according to the needs.

In summary, HTML defines the structure and layout of a web page, while PHP handles the programming logic and server-side data processing. The combination of these two languages allows you to create dynamic and interactive web applications, offering a richer and more personalized user experience.

Opening and closing tags

In PHP, the standard opening and closing tag for starting and ending a block of PHP code is <?php and ?> respectively. Here's how it's used:

```
<?php

// Put your PHP code here

// ...

?>
```

All PHP code you want to run must be enclosed between these two tags. For example, you can define variables, perform operations, call functions, and generate output within this block of code.

The PHP opening and closing tags can also be shortened using the form <? for opening and ?> for closing. However, this shorthand syntax may not be supported in all PHP configurations, so it is recommended that you always use the extended form <?php and ?> for maximum compatibility.

Data types

PHP supports several data types that can be used to store and manipulate information within a program. The main data types in PHP are listed below:

- **Strings**: Strings represent sequences of characters, such as text or words. They can be defined using single quotes (''), double quotes ("") or heredoc syntax. For example: $name = "John";.

- **Numbers**: PHP supports whole numbers (integers) and floating point numbers (floats). Numbers can be used to perform calculations and mathematical operations. For example: $age = 25; $price = 19.99;.

- **Booleans**: Booleans represent truth values and can be only two: true (true) or false (false). Booleans are commonly used in conditional expressions to make decisions in program flow. For example: $isLogged = true;.

- **Arrays**: Arrays allow you to store and organize collections of related values. They can contain elements of different data types and are indexed by keys or by integers. For example: $numbers = array(1, 2, 3, 4, 5);.

- **Objects**: Objects are instances of classes and represent complex entities with properties and methods. Classes define the structure and behavior of objects. Objects are used to build complex and modular data structures. For example:$person = new Person();.

- **Resources**: Resources are special data types that represent external resources such as database connections or open files. Resources are created using specific functions and can be used to interact with external resources. For example:$risorsaDb = mysqli_connect("localhost", "username", "password");.

- **NULL**: NULL is a special data type that indicates no value. It is often used to initialize variables before assigning them a specific value. For example: $variable = NULL;.

In addition to these core data types, PHP also offers more complex data types such as JSON strings, function pointers, and stream resources. You can also create your own data types using user-defined classes and interfaces.

The knowledge of the different data types in PHP is essential for working successfully with variables, expressions and functions in the language.

Comments

Comments are used to annotate source code that is not executed as part of the program. Comments are useful for documentation purposes, to explain how code works, or to temporarily disable portions of code without having to delete them. There are two types of comments in PHP: single line comments and block comments.

Single Line Comments:

Single-line comments begin with two slashes "//" and are used to place short annotations on a single line of code. The text following the two slashes is ignored by PHP during program execution.

Example of a single line comment:

```
// This is a single line comment

echo "Hello, World!";
```

In the example, the single line comment is ignored and does not affect the execution of the "echo" statement.

Block comments:

Block comments start with "/*" and end with "*/". They are used to insert comments across multiple lines or to temporarily disable portions of code that may contain multiple lines.

Block comment example:

```
/*

This is a block comment.

It can span multiple lines.

*/

echo "Hello, World!";
```

In the example, the block comment is ignored and does not affect the execution of the "echo" statement.

It is important to use comments to improve the readability and maintainability of your code. Well-written comments can help developers better understand the code and facilitate collaboration within the development team.

Variables

In PHP, variables are used to store and manipulate data during the execution of a program. A variable in PHP is essentially a container with a name that represents a value or a reference to a value.

Here are some important points to know about variables in PHP:

Declaring a Variable: To declare a variable in PHP, simply use the dollar sign ($) followed by the desired variable name. For example:

```
$name = "Luca";
$and = 25;
```

Assigning a value: To assign a value to a variable, you use the assignment operator (=). For example:

```
$name = "James";
```

Weak Typing: PHP uses weak typing, which means you don't need to declare the type of a variable explicitly. The data type is inferred based on the value assigned to the variable. For example, a variable may hold a string at one time and a number at another:

```
$var = "Hello"; // $var is a string
$var = 42; // $var has become a number
```

String concatenation: To combine variables or text into a string, one can use the concatenation operator (.) in PHP. For example:

```
$name = "James";
$surname = "Smith";
$fullname = $name . " " . $surname;
```

Predefined Variables: PHP offers a number of predefined variables, called superglobals, which contain useful information such as HTTP request parameters, server information, user sessions, and more. For example,$_GET, $_POST, $_SERVER, $_SESSION, are some of the more common superglobal variables that we will look at in more detail later.

Variables in PHP offer a flexible way to store and manipulate data while running a program. You can use them to save user information, calculated values, configurations and more. Variables in PHP are dynamic and allow you to adapt to changes in program flow, giving you great flexibility in developing web applications.

Echo function

In PHP, the echo function is used to display text or variables on the screen or in the output generated by the program. It can be used to directly print content on a web page or display it on the server console, depending on the execution context.

Here are some examples of using the echo function:

Text Printing:

```
echo "Hello, world!";
```

This code will display "Hello, world!" on the screen or in the output.

Printing of variables:

```
$name = "James";

$age = 25;

echo "My name is " . $name . " and I have " . $age . " years.";
```

This code combines the value of the variables $name and $age with text and displays it as output. The dot (.) is used to concatenate strings.

HTML and mixed text:

```
$color = "red";

echo "<h1>My favorite color is " . $color . "!</h1>";
```

In this example, HTML text combined with the value of the $color variable is displayed. The result will be a top-level header with dynamic text.

The echo function is one of the basic functions in PHP for displaying data and variables. It is very useful for generating dynamic output on web pages or displaying debug information on the console.

Error displays

During development, it's natural to make mistakes and encounter challenges in your code. To help you identify and fix these issues, PHP offers an error display mechanism that provides you with valuable debugging information.

To view errors in PHP, you can use the error_reporting() function together with the ini_set() function. Here are some common examples:

View all errors and exceptions:

This is useful during the development phase to identify and fix any errors in the code. Add these lines to the beginning of your PHP script:

```
error_reporting(E_ALL);

ini_set('display_errors', 1);
```

This will set up error reporting on all error types and enable errors to be displayed in the browser.

Hide errors, but log them:

During production, you may want to hide errors from the browser but still log them for debugging or auditing purposes. You can use the following lines:

```
error_reporting(E_ALL & ~E_NOTICE & ~E_DEPRECATED);

ini_set('display_errors', 0);
```

This will set error reporting to all error types except warning messages (E_NOTICE) and deprecated messages (E_DEPRECATED). Errors will be logged in the server error logs, but will not be displayed in the browser.

Custom Error Handling:

You can also handle errors in your own way, for example by logging them in a log file or emailing them to the development manager. You can use the set_error_handler() function to define a custom error handling function. For example:

```
function customErrorHandler($errno, $errstr, $errfile, $errline) {
    // Log or email error information
}

set_error_handler('customErrorHandler');
```

This code will set the customErrorHandler() function as the error handler. You can customize this feature to suit your needs, for example to log errors to a log file or send them via email.

It is important to note that while it is useful to view errors during development, it is advisable to hide them during production for security reasons and not to disclose sensitive information to users. Make sure you disable error viewing in your production environment.

Constants

In PHP, constants are similar to variables, but their value cannot be changed once assigned. Constants are used to store values that should not be changed during program execution.

Here's how to declare and use constants in PHP:

Declaration of a constant: To declare a constant in PHP, you use the function **define()**. The general syntax is as follows:

```
define("CONSTANT_NAME", value, case-insensitive);
```

Where:
- **"CONSTANT_NAME"** is the name of the constant, usually in uppercase.
- **value** is the value assigned to the constant.
- **case-insensitive** is an optional parameter that indicates whether the constant name should be considered case-insensitive (true) or case-sensitive (false). It is set to false by default.

Example:

```
define("PI", 3.14159);

define("NAME", "Sarah Johnson");
```

Accessing constants: To access the value of a constant, just use the constant name without the dollar sign ($). For example:

```
echo PI; // Output: 3.14159

echo NAME; // Output: Sarah Johnson
```

Checking for the existence of a constant: You can check if a constant has been defined using the function defined(). It will return true if the constant exists and false otherwise. Example:

```
if (defined("PI")) {

echo "The constant PI exists.";

} else {

echo "The constant PI does not exist.";

}
```

Predefined Constants: PHP also offers a number of predefined constants that provide useful information, such as PHP_VERSION (PHP version in use), PHP_OS (operating system that PHP runs on), and many others. These constants are already defined in the PHP execution context.

It is good practice to use constants to store values that should not be changed during program execution, such as configuration settings, constant mathematical values, or identification values. Constants provide a way to make your code more readable, maintainable, and reduce the chance of accidental errors in changing values.

Note that the constants are global to the entire PHP script, so they can be used anywhere within the script.

Expressions

PHP expressions are combinations of operators, variables and values that produce a result. They can be used to perform calculations, assign values to variables, compare data, and more.

Assigning a value to a variable:

```
$number = 10;
```

Mathematical calculation:

```
$result = (5 + 3) * 2;
```

String concatenation:

```
$name = "Martha";

$surname = "Blacks";

$fullname = $name . " " . $surname;
```

Value comparison:

```
$number1 = 10;

$number2 = 5;

$greater = ($number1 > $number2);
```

Using functions:

```
$length = strlen("Hello, world!");
```

These are just a few examples of PHP expressions. You can combine operators, variables, and values in many different ways to do the job you want. Expressions are a fundamental part of PHP programming and allow you to manipulate data in various ways.

Operators

In PHP, operators are special symbols used to perform operations on variables and values. They can be classified into different categories, such as arithmetic operators, comparison operators, logical operators and so on. Here is an overview of the main operators available in PHP:

Arithmetic operators:

+	sum
-	subtraction
*	multiplication
/	division
%	remainder of division (form)
**	exponential (raising to a power)

Comparison operators:

==	equal to (value)

===	equals (value and type)
!= or <>	different from (value)
!==	not equal to (value and type)
<	less than
>	greater than
<=	less than or equal to
>=	greater than or equal to

Assignment operators:

=	assigns a value to a variable
+=	sum and assign
-=	subtract and assign
*=	multiply and assign
/=	divide and assign
%=	calculate the remainder of the division and assign
**=	calculate the exponential and assign

Logical operators:

&& or and	And logical
|| or or	Or logical
free	Or logical exclusive
! or not	logical negation

Increment/decrement operators:

++	increment by 1
- -	decrease by 1

There are other operators as well, such as the string concatenation operators (.), the ternary operator (condition ? value1 : value2), the array element access operator ([] or $array[key]) and many others that we will address in the next chapters.

You can combine operators to create complex expressions that perform calculations, comparisons, and other operations. Using the correct operators and understanding their priority (precedence) are important to get the desired results in PHP programming operations.

Arithmetic operators:

```
$a = 10;
$b = 3;

$sum = $a + $b;      // 13
$difference = $a - $b; // 7
$product = $a * $b;   // 30
$quotient = $a / $b;  // 3.333...
$remainder = $a % $b;  // 1
$power = $a ** $b;    // 1000
```

Comparison operators:

```
$a = 5;
$b = 10;

$equal = ($a == $b);       // false
$identical = ($a === $b);    // false
$notEqual = ($a != $b);     // true
$notIdentical = ($a !== $b);  // true
$greaterThan = ($a > $b);    // false
$lessThan = ($a < $b);      // true
$greaterOrEqual = ($a >= $b); // false
$lessOrEqual = ($a <= $b);   // true
```

Assignment operators:

```
$a = 5;
$b = 2;

$a += $b; // $a becomes 7
$b -= 1; // $b becomes 1
$a *= $b; // $a becomes 7
$b /= $a; // $b becomes 0.14285714285714
$a %= 3; // $a becomes 1
```

Logical operators:

```
$a = true;
$b = false;

$andResult = ($a && $b); // false
$orResult = ($a || $b);  // true
$xorResult = ($a xor $b); // true
$notResult = !$a; // false
```

Increment/decrement operators:

```
$a = 5;

$a++; // $a becomes 6
++$a; // $a becomes 7

$b = 10;
$b--; // $b becomes 9
--$b; // $b becomes 8
```

These are just a few examples of how operators can be used in practical situations in PHP. Operators are extremely useful for performing calculations, comparisons, and assignments of values in everyday programming operations.

Control structures and cycles

IF, ELSE

In PHP, the "if-else" control structure is used to execute conditional statements. It allows the program to make decisions based on a condition and execute different blocks of code based on the result of the condition. Here is an example of using the "if-else" structure in PHP:

```php
$number = 10;
if ($number > 5) {
    echo "The number is greater than 5.";
} else {
    echo "The number is less than or equal to 5.";
}
```

In this example, the variable $number is compared to the value 5 using the comparison operator (>). If the condition is true, the first block of code between the curly braces {} is executed, which prints "The number is greater than 5.". If the condition is false, the second block of code in the "else" block is executed, which prints "The number is less than or equal to 5.".

You can also use multiple nested "if-else" clauses to handle more complex conditions. Here is an example:

```php
$number = 10;

if ($number > 10) {
    echo "The number is greater than 10.";
} elseif ($number < 10) {
    echo "The number is less than 10.";
} else {
    echo "The number equals 10.";
}
```

In this case, several conditions are evaluated. If the number is greater than 10, "The number is greater than 10." is printed. If the number is less than 10, "The number is less than 10." is printed. If none of the above conditions are true, the "else" block is executed and "The number equals 10." is printed.

The "if-else" structure can be used to handle more complex conditional decisions within your PHP code.

Switch statement

In PHP, the "switch" statement is used to perform a series of comparisons and take different actions based on the result of those comparisons. It is an alternative form of control structure to the "if-elseif-else" set of clauses when evaluating a variable against several values. Here is an example of using the "switch" statement in PHP:

```php
$day = "Monday";
```

```
switch ($day) {
  case "Monday":
    echo "Today is Monday.";
    break;
  case "Tuesday":
    echo "Today is Tuesday.";
    break;
  case "Wednesday":
    echo "Today is Wednesday.";
    break;
  case "Thursday":
    echo "Today is Thursday.";
    break;
  case "Friday":
    echo "Today is Friday.";
    break;
  default:
    echo "Today is not a day of the week.";
}
```

In this example, the variable $day is evaluated against several cases using the "switch" statement. If the value of $day matches one of the cases, the code block corresponding to that case is executed, followed by the "break" statement to exit the "switch" statement. If the value of $day does not match any of the cases, the "default" case code block is executed.

When a matching case is found, the corresponding statements are executed, but it is important to remember to use the "break" statement at the end of each case to prevent code blocks from subsequent cases from being executed as well.

The "switch" statement can be useful when you need to make multiple comparisons and want to perform different actions based on the value of the variable.

Ternary operator

The ternary (or conditional) operator is a syntactic shorthand for writing simple conditions concisely. It consists of a conditional expression that returns a value based on the result of the condition. The ternary operator is represented by the following syntax:

```
condition ? value_if_true : value_if_false;
```

If the condition is true, the value "value_if_true" is returned, otherwise the value "value_if_false" is returned. Here is an example of using the ternary operator in PHP:

```
$and = 20;

$result = ($age >= 18) ? "Adult" : "Minor";

echo $result;
```

In this example, the condition $age >= 18 is evaluated. If the condition is true, the value "age" is assigned to the variable $result. If the condition is false, the value "Minor" is assigned. Then, the value of the $result variable is printed, which will be "Adult" if the age is greater than or equal to 18, otherwise it will be "Minor".

The ternary operator can be very useful for writing simple conditions more concisely, avoiding the need to use the "if-else" checking structure for simple cases. However, it's important to use it sparingly and make sure your code remains readable and understandable.

For, while e do

In PHP, there are three types of loops for iterating through a block of code repeatedly: the "for" loop, the "while" loop, and the "do-while" loop. Here's how they work:

Cycle "**for**":

The "for" loop is used when the number of iterations needed is known in advance. It has the following syntax:

```
for (initialization; condition; increment/decrement) {
    // Block of code to execute
}
```

Example of using the "for" loop:

```
for ($i = 0; $i < 5; $i++) {
    echo $i;
}
```

In this example, the "for" loop runs until the variable $i is less than 5. At each iteration, the value of $i is printed. The variable $i is initialized to 0 and is incremented by 1 at each iteration ($i++).

Cycle "**while**":

The "while" loop is used when you don't know the exact number of iterations needed in advance. It has the following syntax:

```
while (condition) {
    // Block of code to execute
}
```

Example of using the "while" loop:

```
$i = 0;
while ($i < 5) {
    echo $i;
    $i++;
}
```

In this example, the "while" loop runs until the variable $i is less than 5. Inside the loop, the value of $i is printed and then incremented by 1 ($i++).

Cycle "**do-while**":

The "do-while" loop is similar to the "while" loop, but executes the block of code at least once before evaluating the condition. It has the following syntax:

```
do {
    // Block of code to execute
} while (condition);
```

Example of using the "do-while" loop:

```
$i = 0;
do {
    echo $i;
    $i++;
} while ($i < 5);
```

In this example, the "do-while" loop runs at least once, regardless of the condition. The value of $i is printed and then incremented by 1. The loop runs until the condition $i < 5 is true.

Both the "while" loop and the "do-while" loop continue executing the block of code as long as the specified condition is true. In case the condition is never true, the loops will continue indefinitely, creating an endless loop. Therefore, it is important to ensure that the condition occurs at some point or to use proper logic to avoid unwanted infinite loops.

Break and continue

The break and continue statements are used to control the flow of execution within a loop (such as for, while, do-while or foreach).

The instruction **break** is used to stop the execution of the loop immediately and exit the loop. It is often used when a specific condition is met and you want to terminate the iteration of the loop.

Example of using break:

```
for ($i = 0; $i < 10; $i++) {
    if ($i == 5) {
        break;
    }
    echo $i . " ";
}
```

In this example, the for loop runs from 0 to 9. When the variable $i becomes 5, the break statement runs, immediately terminating the loop. Therefore, the numbers 0 to 4 will be printed, but the loop stops when $i becomes 5.

The output will be:

```
0 1 2 3 4
```

The instruction **continue** is used to skip the current iteration of the loop and move on to the next one. It is often used when you want to temporarily skip an iteration without completely terminating the loop.

Example of using continue:

```
for ($i = 0; $i < 10; $i++) {
    if ($i % 2 == 0) {
        continue;
    }
    echo $i . " ";
}
```

In this example, the for loop runs from 0 to 9. When the variable $i is an even number (divisible by 2), the continue statement runs, skipping the current iteration and moving on to the next. Therefore, only odd numbers will be printed.

The output will be:

```
1 3 5 7 9
```

Using break and continue allows you to control the flow of execution within a loop based on specific conditions. It is useful for handling special cases or for optimizing code when some iterations need to be skipped or the loop needs to be stopped early.

Texts and strings

PHP functions for string manipulation

There are many built-in functions for string manipulation. These functions allow you to perform operations such as substring search, text replacement, case conversion, formatting, and much more. Here are some examples of string manipulation functions in PHP:

strlen($string): Returns the length of a string.

```
$string = "Hello, World!";
$length = strlen($string);
echo $length; // Outputs: 13
```

strpos($string, $substring): Returns the position of the first occurrence of a substring within a string. If the substring is not found, return false.

```
$string = "Hello, World!";
$position = strpos($string, "World");
echo $position; // Outputs: 7
```

substr($string, $start, $length): Returns a substring of a string, starting at the specified position $start and for an optional length $length.

```
$string = "Hello, World!";
$substring = substr($string, 0, 5);
echo $substring; // Outputs: Hello
```

str_replace($replace, $with, $string): Replaces all occurrences of a substring with another substring within a string.

```
$string = "Hello, World!";
$newString = str_replace("World", "PHP", $string);
echo $newString;  // Output: Hello, PHP!
```

strtolower($string): Convert a string to lowercase.

```
$string = "Hello, World!";
$stringLowercase = strtolower($string);
echo $stringLowercase;  // Output: hello, world!
```

strtoupper($string): Converts a string to uppercase.

```
$string = "Hello, World!";
```

```
$stringUppercase = strtoupper($string);
echo $stringUppercase;  // Output: HELLO, WORLD!
```

These are just a few examples of string manipulation functions available in PHP. The official PHP documentation provides a complete list of string manipulation functions along with detailed examples.

String formatting

PYou want to use different functions to format strings in different ways. Here are some examples of string formatting in PHP:

sprintf($format, $arg1, $arg2, ...): Returns a string formatted according to the specified format and supplied arguments.

```
$name = "John";

$and = 25;

$formatted = sprintf("My name is %s and I'm %d.", $name, $age);

echo $formatted; // Output: My name is John and I'm 25 years old.
```

number_format($number, $decimals, $thousandseparator, $decimalseparator): Returns a formatted string of a number with the specified number of decimals and separators for thousands and decimals.

```
$number = 12345.6789;

$formatted = number_format($number, 2, ",", ".");

echo $formatted; // Outputs: 12,345.68
```

ucfirst($stringa): Returns a string with the first character converted to uppercase.

```
$string = "hello, world!";

$formatted = ucfirst($string);

echo $formatted; // Outputs: Hello, world!
```

ucwords($stringa): Returns a string with the first character of each word converted to uppercase.

```
$string = "hello, world!";

$formatted = ucwords($string);
```

```
echo $formatted; // Outputs: Hello, World!
```

str_pad($string, $length, $pad, $pad_position): Returns a string with a specified length, adding the specified padding character to the beginning or end of the string.

```
$string = "Hello";

$formattedString = str_pad($stringa, 10, "*", STR_PAD_BOTH);

echo $formattedString;  // Output: **Hello***
```

These are just a few examples of string formatting in PHP. There are many other functions available to manipulate and format strings to suit your needs. See the official PHP documentation for more details on string formatting functions.

In particular, with regard to the sprintf() function, there are several formats that can be used to format strings. Here are some common formatting formats:

%s: Used to enter a string.

```
$name = "John";

$formatted = sprintf("Hello, %s!", $name);

echo $formatted; // Output: Hi, John!
```

%d or **%i**: Used to enter an integer.

```
$age = 25;

$formatted = sprintf("You are %d years old.", $age);

echo $formatted; // Output: You are 25 years old.
```

%f: Used to enter a decimal number.

```
$pi = 3.14159;

$formatted = sprintf("The value of pi is %f.", $pi);

echo $formatted; // Output: The value of pi is 3.141590.
```

%.2f: Used to enter a decimal number with a specific precision.

```
$pi = 3.14159;

$formatted = sprintf("The value of pi is %.2f.", $pi);

echo $formatted; // Output: The value of pi is 3.14.
```

%b: Used to enter an integer in binary format.

```
$number = 10;

$formatted = sprintf("The number %d in binary is %b.", $number, $number);

echo $formatted; // Output: The number 10 in binary is 1010.
```

These are just a few examples of string formatting formats used with the sprintf() function. You can combine these formats with other control characters and width and precision specifications to achieve more complex and customized results. You can refer to the official PHP documentation for more details on supported string formatting formats.

String comparison

You can use comparison operators to compare strings. Here are some common string comparison operators:

== (equality): Returns true if the two strings are equal.

```
$string1 = "Hello";
$string2 = "hello";
if ($string1 == $string2) {
    echo "Strings are equal.";
} else {
    echo "Strings are different.";
}
```

!= or **<>** (inequality): Returns true if the two strings are different.

```
$string1 = "Hello";
$string2 = "World";
if ($string1 != $string2) {
    echo "Strings are different.";
} else {
    echo "Strings are equal.";
}
```

=== (strict equality): Returns true if the two strings are equal in both value and type.

```
$string1 = "123";
$string2 = "123";
if ($string1 === $string2) {
    echo "Strings are equal in value and type.";
} else {
    echo "Strings are different in value or type.";
}
```

< (less than) and > (greater than): Return true if the first string is less than or greater than the second string respectively based on alphabetical order.

```
$string1 = "Apple";
$string2 = "Banana";
if ($string1 < $string2) {
    echo "String 1 comes before string 2.";
} else {
    echo "String 1 comes after string 2.";
}
```

<= (less than or equal to) and >= (greater than or equal to): Return true if the first string is less than or equal to, or greater than or equal to, respectively, the second string based on alphabetical order.

```
$string1 = "Apple";
$string2 = "Banana";
if ($string1 <= $string2) {
    echo "String 1 comes before or equal to string 2.";
} else {
    echo "String 1 comes after string 2.";
}
```

Please note that string comparison can be affected by character encoding and locale settings, it is important to consider some specific aspects to get correct and predictable results. Here are some important considerations for an in-depth string comparison in PHP:

Case sensitivity: By default, PHP is case-sensitive when comparing strings. This means that uppercase and lowercase letters are considered different. For example, the strings "Hello" and "hello" are different.

```
$string1 = "Hello";
$string2 = "hello";
if ($string1 == $string2) {
    echo "Strings are equal.";
} else {
    echo "Strings are different.";
}
```

Output: Strings are different.

To perform a case-insensitive comparison, you can use the strcasecmp() function or convert both strings to a specific case, for example using strtolower() or strtoupper().

Unicode and character encodings: If the strings contain Unicode characters or are encoded in a specific character set, there may be differences in the comparison due to different character representations. Make sure that strings are encoded in the same character set and consider using functions like mb_strtolower() or mb_strtoupper() to handle Unicode characters correctly.

Whitespace and Control Characters: Strings may contain leading or trailing whitespace or invisible control characters which can affect the comparison. You can remove whitespace using the trim() function and check for specific characters using functions like strpos() or preg_match().

Length and Partial Comparison: When comparing strings, you may want to perform a partial comparison, such as checking if one string is contained in another. You can use functions like strpos() or strstr() to check for a substring.

```
$string1 = "Hello, World!";
$string2 = "Hello";
if (strpos($string1, $string2) !== false) {
    echo "String 2 is contained in string 1.";
} else {
    echo "String 2 is not contained in string 1.";
}
```

Output: String 2 is contained in string 1.

Strict equality: If you need to verify that two strings are identical in both value and type, you can use the strict equality operator ===. This comparison takes into account both the value and data type of the strings.

```
$string1 = "123";
$string2 = "123";
if ($string1 === $string2) {
    echo "Strings are equal in value and type.";
} else {
    echo "Strings are different in value or type.";
}
```

Output: Strings are equal in value and type.

Considering these aspects can help you get correct and predictable results when comparing strings in PHP. It is important to adapt the approach to the specific case, taking into account the characteristics of the strings involved in the comparison.

Date and time

You can use different functions to work with dates and time. Here are some examples:

date(): The date() function returns the date and/or time formatted according to the supplied parameters. Here are some examples:

```
echo date('Y-m-d'); // Output: 2023-05-23 (current date in "year-month-day" format)
echo date('H:i:s'); // Output: 14:30:45 (current time in the format "hour:minutes:seconds")
echo date('Y-m-d H:i:s'); // Output: 2023-05-23 14:30:45 (current date and time in the format "year-month-day hour:minutes:seconds")
```

time(): The time() function returns the current UNIX timestamp, which represents the number of seconds since January 1, 1970 at 00:00:00 UTC. You can use the date() function to format the timestamp into a readable date:

```
$timestamp = time();
echo date('Y-m-d H:i:s', $timestamp);  // Output: 2023-05-23 14:30:45 (current date and time)
```

strtotime(): The strtotime() function converts a text string into a UNIX timestamp. It can be used to analyze specific dates and times:

```
$timestamp = strtotime('2023-05-23');
echo date('Y-m-d', $timestamp);  // Output: 2023-05-23

$timestamp = strtotime('tomorrow');
echo date('Y-m-d', $timestamp); // Output: tomorrow's date

$timestamp = strtotime('+1 week');
echo date('Y-m-d', $timestamp); // Output: date in one week
```

gmdate(): The gmdate() function returns the date and/or time formatted according to the supplied parameters, using the GMT (Greenwich Mean Time) timezone:

```
echo gmdate('Y-m-d H:i:s'); // Output: 2023-05-23 12:30:45 (current date and time in GMT format)
```

microtime(): The microtime() function returns the current time with microsecond precision. It can be used to measure the execution time of a piece of code:

```
$start = microtime(true);

// Code to measure

$fine = microtime(true);
$runtime = $end - $start;
echo "Execution time: " . $runtime . " seconds";
```

You can use these functions together with other functions of the DateTime class to perform more complex operations such as calculating differences between dates, handling time zones, etc.

Regular expressions

Regular expressions, also called regex, are a powerful tool for manipulating text in PHP. They allow for string matching and manipulation based on specific patterns. Here are some examples of how to use regular expressions in PHP:

preg_match(): The preg_match() function is used to search for a pattern match within a string. Returns true if a match is found, false otherwise.

```
$string = "Hello, World!";
if (preg_match('/Hello/', $stringa)) {
    echo "Match found!";
} else {
    echo "Match not found.";
}
```

preg_replace(): The preg_replace() function is used to replace matching patterns with another string within an input string.

```
$string = "Hello, World!";
$newString = preg_replace('/World/', 'PHP', $string);
echo $newString;  // Output: Hello, PHP!
```

Regular Expression Modifiers: PHP supports several ways to use regular expressions, called modifiers, that allow you to influence the behavior of matches. For example, the "i" modifier indicates a case-insensitive match.

```
$string = "Hello, World!";
if (preg_match('/hello/i', $stringa)) {
    echo "Case-insensitive match found!";
} else {
    echo "No case-insensitive match found.";
}
```

Special characters and quantifiers: Regular expressions in PHP can include special characters and quantifiers to specify more complex patterns. For example, the dot "." matches any character, the asterisk "*" matches zero or more occurrences of the previous character, and the "?" makes the match optional.

```php
$string = "Hello, World!";
if (preg_match('/W.rld/', $stringa)) {
    echo "Match found!";
} else {
    echo "Match not found.";
}
```

Array

Arrays

Arrays in PHP are very versatile data structures that allow you to store and manipulate sets of related values. An array can contain zero or more elements, which can be any data type supported (in our case) by PHP, such as strings, numbers, booleans, objects, or even other arrays. Here are some basic concepts related to arrays in PHP:

Declaring an array: You can declare an array using array syntax, which consists of defining a variable followed by square brackets. You can assign values to the array during declaration or later using the = assignment operator.

```
$fruit = array("Apple", "Banana", "Orange");
```

Accessing elements of an array: Elements of an array are accessed using the corresponding indexes. Array indices start at 0 for the first element.

```
echo $fruit[0]; // Output: Apple

echo $fruit[1]; // Outputs: Banana

echo $fruit[2]; // Output: Orange
```

Adding elements to the array: You can add elements to the array using the syntax of indexes in square brackets.

```
$fruit[] = "Pear"; // Add "Pear" as a new element to the array

$fruit[3] = "Kiwi"; // Add "Kiwi" as an element at index 3 of the array
```

Editing Array Elements: You can edit an array element by assigning a new value to the corresponding index.

```
$fruit[1] = "Pineapple"; // Change the element at index 1 to the value "Pineapple"
```

Removing elements from the array: You can remove an element from the array using the unset() function by specifying the index of the element to remove.

```
unset($fruit[2]); // Remove the element at index 2 from the array
```

Associative arrays

Associative arrays are a special type of array in PHP where elements are associated with keys instead of numerical indexes. Instead of using numeric indexes as in numbered arrays, associative arrays use keys which can be strings or integer values. Keys act as identifiers for array elements and allow for more intuitive access to values.

Here is an example of declaring an associative array in PHP:

```
$person = array(
    'name' => 'John',
    'age' => 25,
    'profession' => 'Programmer'
);
```

In this example, we have defined an associative array called $person with three elements. The element keys are 'name', 'age' and 'profession', while the corresponding values are 'John', 25 and 'Programmer'. It is important to note that keys are delimited by single or double quotes.

You can access the elements of an associative array using their respective keys:

```
echo $person['name']; // Output: John

echo $person['age']; // Outputs: 25

echo $person['profession']; // Outputs: Programmer
```

You can also edit or assign new values to items using their respective keys:

```
$person['age'] = 30; // Change value of element with key 'age'

$person['gender'] = 'Male'; // Add a new element with key 'sex'
```

You can use PHP's array manipulation functions to work with associative arrays. For example, the array_keys() function returns an array containing all the keys in an associative array, while the array_values() function returns an array containing all the values.

```
$keys = array_keys($person); // Return an array containing the keys

$values = array_values($person); // Return an array containing the values
```

Associative arrays are especially useful when working with structured data or when you need to identify array elements by meaningful names or identifiers. They allow you to organize and access data more intuitively and readably than numbered arrays.

Functions dedicated to arrays

PHP provides a variety of dedicated functions for working with arrays. These functions simplify and streamline common array manipulation operations. Here are some of the most used functions:

count(): Returns the number of elements in an array.

```
$fruits = array('Apple', 'Banana', 'Orange');
$numberElements = count($fruits); // Returns 3
```

array_push(): Adds one or more elements to the end of an array.

```
$fruits = array('Apple', 'Banana');
array_push($fruits, 'Orange', 'Kiwi'); // $fruits becomes array('Apple', 'Banana', 'Orange', 'Kiwi')
```

array_pop(): Remove and return the last element of an array.

```
$fruits = array('Apple', 'Banana', 'Orange');
$lastItem = array_pop($fruits); // $fruits becomes array('Apple', 'Banana'), $lastItem becomes 'Orange'
```

array_shift(): Remove and return the first element of an array.

```
$fruits = array('Apple', 'Banana', 'Orange');
$firstItem = array_shift($fruits); // $fruits becomes array('Banana', 'Orange'), $firstItem becomes 'Apple'
```

array_unshift(): Adds one or more elements to the beginning of an array.

```
$fruits = array('Banana', 'Orange');
array_unshift($fruits, 'Apple', 'Kiwi'); // $fruits becomes array('Apple', 'Kiwi', 'Banana', 'Orange')
```

array_merge(): Merges two or more arrays into a new array.

```
$fruits1 = array('Apple', 'Banana');
$fruits2 = array('Orange', 'Kiwi');
$fruitsTotal = array_merge($fruits1, $fruits2); // $fruitsTotal becomes array('Apple', 'Banana', 'Orange', 'Kiwi')
```

7. **array_reverse()**: Reverse the order of the elements of an array.

```
$fruits = array('Apple', 'Banana', 'Orange');
$fruitsReversed = array_reverse($fruit); // $fruitsReversed becomes array('Orange', 'Banana', 'Apple')
```

There are many other useful functions like array_slice(), array_splice(), array_filter(), array_map(), array_search(), array_keys(), array_values(), which allow you to perform specific operations on arrays efficiently.

Array cycles

We have two common ways to iterate over the elements of an array: using the for loop or the foreach loop. Both loops have slightly different purposes and syntax and can be used according to your specific needs.

The **for loop** is a control loop based on a numeric index. It is usually used when you want to access array elements based on their numerical index. Here's an example of using the for loop to iterate over the elements of an array:

```
$fruits = array('Apple', 'Banana', 'Orange');

for ($i = 0; $i < count($fruits); $i++) {
    echo $fruits[$i] . '<br>';
}
```

The for loop uses a control variable ($i in the example) to keep track of the current index. The termination condition ($i < count($fruit)) checks if the index is less than the total number of elements in the array. With each iteration, the index is incremented and the corresponding element is accessed using the index.

On the other hand, the foreach loop is specifically designed to iterate over the elements of an array without having to manually manage indexes. It is especially useful when you only want to access element values and not indexes. Here's an example of using the foreach loop to iterate over the elements of an array:

```
$fruits = array('Apple', 'Banana', 'Orange');

foreach ($fruits as $item) {
    echo $item . '<br>';
}
```

The **foreach loop** automatically iterates over all the elements of the array without needing to explicitly specify indexes. In each iteration, the current value of the element is assigned to the temporary variable ($element in the example) and can be used within the loop block.

In general, the for loop is more flexible and can be used to control iteration based on custom conditions, change indexes, or perform specific operations. The foreach loop, on the other hand, is simpler and more convenient to use when you just want to access element values without having to manually manage indexes.

Choosing between the for loop and the foreach loop depends on the specific needs of your code and the iteration logic you plan to implement.

Multidimensional arrays

Arrays in PHP can be multidimensional, which means they can contain other arrays as elements. In other words, each element of a multidimensional array is itself an array. This allows you to create complex, nested data structures, such as arrays or tables.

You can declare a multidimensional array in PHP in several ways. Here is an example:

```
$matrix = array(
    array(1, 2, 3),
    array(4, 5, 6),
    array(7, 8, 9)
);
```

In this example, we have declared a 3x3 matrix, where each element is an array of integers. You can access multidimensional array elements using multiple indexes. For example, to access the element in row 2, column 1 (the value 4), you could use the indexing $array[1][0].

You can also iterate over multidimensional arrays using nested loops, such as a nested for loop or a nested foreach loop. For example:

```
$matrix = array(
    array(1, 2, 3),
    array(4, 5, 6),
    array(7, 8, 9)
);

// Iteration using a nested for loop
for ($i = 0; $i < count($matrix); $i++) {
    for ($j = 0; $j < count($matrix[$i]); $j++) {
        echo $matrix[$i][$j] . ' ';
    }
    echo '<br>';
}

// Iterating using a nested foreach loop
foreach ($matrix as $row) {
    foreach ($row as $item) {
        echo $item . ' ';
    }
    echo '<br>';
}
```

These loops allow you to visit each element of the multidimensional array and perform specific operations on them.

Multidimensional arrays in PHP can have more than two dimensions. You can create even more complex data structures by adding nested arrays within other nested arrays.

Data validation

For array validation in PHP, you can use different techniques depending on the specific requirements of your use case. Here are some common approaches to validating arrays:

Checking for the existence of keys:

You can check if a specific key exists in an array using the array_key_exists() function or the isset() operator.

```
$data = array(
  'name' => 'John',
  'age' => 30,
  'email' => 'john@example.com'
);
if (array_key_exists('name', $data)) {
  // Key 'name' exists in array $data
}
if (isset($data['age'])) {
  // The 'age' key exists in the $data array and is set
}
```

Checking the value type:

You can check if an array element is of a specific type using the corresponding is_* function (e.g. is_string(), is_numeric(), is_array(), etc.).

```
if (is_string($data['name'])) {
  // The element corresponding to key 'name' is a string
}
if (is_numeric($data['age'])) {
  // The element corresponding to the 'age' key is a number
}
```

Verification of data validity:

You can use specific functions to validate the data according to the desired criteria. For example, to validate an email address, you can use the filter_var() function with the FILTER_VALIDATE_EMAIL filter.

```
$email = 'john@example.com';
if (filter_var($email, FILTER_VALIDATE_EMAIL)) {
  // The email address is valid
}
```

Custom validation:

If you have more complex validation requirements, you can implement custom rules using if conditions and custom validation functions.

```
$data = array(
  'name' => 'John',
  'age' => 30
);
if (isset($data['name']) && is_string($data['name']) && strlen($data['name']) >= 2) {
  // Key 'name' exists, is a string and has at least 2 characters
}
```

Validating arrays depends heavily on your specific needs and the criteria that need to be met. Several techniques can be combined to achieve a more complete and accurate validation of the data in the array.

Functions

Functions

Functions are reusable blocks of code that allow you to organize and subdivide your code into logical, modular units. Functions in PHP can be user-defined (custom functions) or they can be predefined functions provided by the language.

Here is an example of a custom function in PHP:

```php
function sayHello($name) {
    echo "Hello, $name!";
}
sayHello("Anthony"); // Output: Hello, Anthony!
```

In the example above, we defined a function called sayHello() that takes a parameter $name. Within the body of the function, the echo statement is used to display the message on the screen. The function is called later, passing the name "Anthony".

It is also possible to define functions with optional parameters and default values. For example:

```php
function sayHello($name = "Anonymous") {
    echo "Hello, $name!";
}
sayHello(); // Output: Hello, Anonymous!
sayHello("Anthony"); // Output: Hello, Anthony!
```

In the example above, the parameter $name of the hello() function has a default value of "Anonymous". If the function is called without supplying an argument, the default value will be used. If an argument is supplied, the supplied value will override the default value.

Functions in PHP are a powerful way to organize your code, improve the readability and maintainability of your code, as well as promote code reuse. You can define your own custom functions to implement logic specific to your program or use the many predefined functions available to simplify common operations.

Recursive functions

A recursive function is a function that calls itself within its body. This recursive calling mechanism allows you to solve complex problems by breaking them into smaller subproblems.

Recursive functions must have a base condition (or exit condition) that determines when the recursive call should stop. Without a proper ground condition, the function could keep calling itself indefinitely, resulting in an out-of-memory (infinite recursion) error.

Here is an example of a recursive function in PHP to calculate the factorial of a number:

```
function factorial($n) {
    if ($n == 0) {
        return 1; // basic condition: the factorial of 0 is 1
    } else {
        return $n * factorial($n - 1); // recursive call
    }
}

$number = 5;
$result = factorial($number);
echo "Factorial of $number is $result"; // Output: The factorial of 5 is 120
```

In the example above, the factorial() function calculates the factorial of a given number. The basic condition is when the number passed to the function becomes 0, in which case the function returns 1. Otherwise, the function calls itself with a number reduced by 1 and multiplies the current number by the result of the recursive call.

It is important to ensure that a recursive function always reaches the ground condition so that the recursive call fails and the program does not enter an infinite loop.

Recursive functions can be used to solve a variety of problems, such as processing nested data structures (such as trees or graphs), generating sequences (such as the Fibonacci sequence), exploring paths, or solving divide-and-conquer problems.

However, care must be taken when using recursive functions, as they can consume a lot of memory and execution time if used inefficiently or with large data. Therefore, it is important to understand the logic and handling of recursion well before using it appropriately.

Visibility of variables

The visibility (or scope) of variables in functions is determined by where they are declared. Variables can be of three visibility types: global, local, and static.

Global variables: Global variables are declared outside of any function and are accessible throughout the PHP script. They can be used inside any function without having to re-declare them. Here is an example of a global variable:

```php
$name = "Anthony";

function sayHello() {
    global $name; // use the global variable inside the function
    echo "Hello, $name!";
}

sayHello(); // Output: Hello, Anthony!
```

Local variables: Local variables are declared inside a function and are only accessible inside that function. They exist only during the execution of the function and are destroyed once the function is finished. Here is an example of a local variable:

```php
function sayHello() {
    $name = "Anthony"; // local variable
    echo "Hello, $name!";
}

sayHello(); // Output: Hello, Anthony!
echo $name; // Will throw an error: undefined variable
```

The variable $name is declared inside the say hello() function and is only accessible inside that function. It cannot be used outside of the function.

Static variables: Static variables are local variables that keep their value even after the function has finished executing. They are initialized only once and their value is preserved between subsequent calls to the function. Here is an example of a static variable:

```php
function callCounter() {
    static $counter = 0; // static variable
    $counter++;
    echo "Number of calls: $counter<br>";
}

callCounter(); // Output: Number of calls: 1
callCounter(); // Output: Number of calls: 2
callCounter(); // Output: Number of calls: 3
```

In the example above, the variable $counter is declared as static: it therefore retains its value between successive calls to the function callCounter().

Proper management of variable visibility is important to avoid conflicts, improve code readability, and ensure that variables are only accessible when needed. We recommend using local variables whenever possible and limiting the use of global variables, as they can cause unwanted side effects and make your code more difficult to understand and maintain.

Pass by value or by reference

Passing parameters to functions can be done by value or by reference. This determines how data passed to functions is treated and whether changes within the function affect the original value of the data.

Pass by value: By default, PHP uses pass by value. This means that when you pass a variable by value to a function, a separate copy of the variable is created within the function. Changes made to the variable inside the function do not affect the original variable outside the function. Here is an example:

```
function increment($number) {
    $number++;
    echo "Value inside function: $number<br>";
}
$value = 5;
increment($value); // Output: Value inside the function: 6
echo "Value outside function: $value"; // Output: Value outside the function: 5
```

In the example above, the increment() function receives the parameter $number for value. A copy of the variable $value is created and incremented within the function. However, the original value of $value outside the function remains unchanged.

Pass by reference: Parameters can be passed by reference by using the & operator before the parameter name. In this case, instead of creating a separate copy of the variable, a reference to the original variable is passed to the function. Changes made to the variable within the function directly affect the original variable. Here is an example:

```
function increment(&$number) {
    $number++;
    echo "Value inside function: $number<br>";
}
$value = 5;
increment($value); // Output: Value inside the function: 6
echo "Value outside function: $value"; // Output: Value outside the function: 6
```

In the example above, the increment() function receives the parameter $number by reference. The reference to the variable $value is passed, so changes made within the function are reflected directly on the original variable.

It is important to note that passing by reference can have unwanted side effects, as changes made within the function can affect other parts of the code that share the same variable. Therefore, you should only use the pass by reference when necessary and when you are aware of the consequences.

To summarize, passing by value creates a separate copy of the variable inside the function, while passing by reference passes a reference to the original variable. You can choose the appropriate passing method according to the needs of your code.

PHP methods

HTTP requests

In computing, a HTTP (Hypertext Transfer Protocol) request is a message sent by a client (such as a web browser) to a web server in order to request a resource. The HTTP protocol is the main protocol used for communication between clients and servers in the context of the World Wide Web.

In PHP, HTTP requests are handled using the superglobals $_GET, $_POST, $_REQUEST, $_SERVER and others. These variables contain information about the data sent from the client to the server and can be used to get parameters, form data, HTTP headers and more.

GET and POST

$_GET and $_POST are two superglobal variables used to access the data sent to the server through an HTTP GET and POST request respectively.

$_GET:

- Contains the parameters passed through the URL in the form name=value after the question mark.

- The parameters are visible in the URL and can be reported to search engines.

- It is limited in the amount of data it can carry (usually less than 8KB).

Usage example:

```
// Example URL: http://example.com/page.php?name=Mark&age=25
$name = $_GET['name']; // Mark
$age = $_GET[age]; // 25
```

$_POST:

- Contains data submitted via an HTML form using the POST method.

- The parameters are not visible in the URL.

- It can carry a larger amount of data than $_GET.

Usage example:

```
// HTML form example:
// <form method="post" action="page.php">
//     <input type="text" name="name">
//     <input type="text" name="age">
//     <input type="submit" value="Send">
```

```
// </form>

$name = $_POST['name']; // value of the "name" field of the form
$age = $_POST[age]; // value of the "age" field of the form
```

It is important to note that both $_GET and $_POST are associative arrays that contain data sent from the client to the server. You need to be careful about security when using the data received from these variables, for example by filtering and processing the data correctly to prevent attacks such as SQL injection or cross-site scripting (XSS).

Manage Cookies

Cookies are used to store client (browser) information in the form of key-value pairs. Cookies are sent from the server to the client via HTTP headers and can be used to maintain session state, store user preferences, track user activity and more.

Here's how to manage cookies in PHP:

Set a cookie:
To set a cookie, use the setcookie() function, which sets an HTTP header to send the cookie to the client. The general syntax is as follows:

```
setcookie(name, value, expiration, path, domain, security, httponly);
```

- **name**: The name of the cookie.

- **value**: The value associated with the cookie.

- **expiration** (optional): The expiration date of the cookie. It can be a Unix timestamp or a specific date format. If omitted, the cookie will expire when the browser is closed.

- **path** (optional): The path on the server where the cookie will be valid. If set to "/", the cookie will be valid for the entire domain.

- **domain** (optional): The domain for which the cookie will be valid. If not specified, the cookie will only be valid for the current domain.

- **security** (optional): Indicates whether the cookie should be transmitted over a secure HTTPS connection. The default is false.

- **httponly** (optional): Indicates whether the cookie should be accessible only through HTTP and not through JavaScript. The default is false.

Example of setting a cookie:

```
setcookie("name", "Mark", time() + 3600, "/");
```

Read a cookie:
To read a cookie, use the $_COOKIE variable, which is an associative array containing all the cookies sent by the client. You can access the value of a specific cookie by using its name as a key in the $_COOKIE array. Example of reading a cookie:

```
$name = $_COOKIE["name"];
```

Edit a cookie:
To edit a cookie, you simply set the cookie again using the setcookie() function with the new desired values. Note that cookies are sent to the client as HTTP headers and, therefore, to modify an existing cookie you must set the cookie again before sending any output to the client.

Delete a cookie:
To delete a cookie, you can use the setcookie() function with an expiration value passed in the past or set the cookie with an empty value. For example:

```
setcookie("name", "", time() - 3600, "/");
```

It is important to note that cookies are saved on the client side and sent to the server with each subsequent HTTP request. Because cookies can be modified by the client, you shouldn't store sensitive information.

Manage sessions

Sessions in PHP are a mechanism that allows data to be stored persistently between different client requests. Unlike cookies, which are stored on the client side, sessions are managed by the server.

Sessions therefore offer a convenient way to manage user state across various HTTP requests and allow information to be kept persistent without having to depend on cookies or send sensitive data to the client.

When a session is started, PHP creates a unique session identifier (called the session ID) which is associated with the client. The session identifier is usually stored in a cookie sent to the client, but can also be transmitted via URL. Subsequently, the session data is stored on the server and can be accessed and changed during subsequent requests.

Here are the basic steps to manage sessions in PHP:

Starting a session: To start a session, you need to call the session_start() function. This function initializes or restores the existing session, if any. It is important to call session_start() at the beginning of any PHP script that requires the use of sessions.

```
session_start() ;
```

Saving data in the session: You can save data in the session by assigning it to variables in the $_SESSION associative array. For example:

```
$_SESSION['variable_name'] = $value;
```

Retrieving session data: You can access session data by reading the variables in the $_SESSION array. For example:

```
$value = $_SESSION['variable_name'];
```

Editing session data: You can edit session data by assigning new values to variables in the $_SESSION array.

```
$_SESSION['variable_name'] = $new_value;
```

Unsetting data from the session: To unset a variable from the session, you can use the unset() operator or the session_unset() function. For example:

```
unset($_SESSION['variable_name']);
```

Closing the session: When you are done using the session, you can close it by calling the session_destroy() function. This deletes all session data from the server and invalidates the session identifier. The session can be started again with session_start().

```
session_destroy() ;
```

It is important to note that sessions in PHP require a storage mechanism to be configured, which can be file-based, database-based, or other custom storage methods. The default configuration stores session data in files on the server.

REQUEST e SERVER

$_REQUEST and $_SERVER are two superglobals used to access HTTP request data and server information.

$_REQUEST:

-   Contains data sent to the server via an HTTP request, including data sent with both the GET method and the POST method.

-   Combine data from $_GET, $_POST and $_COOKIE.

-   You can use it to access parameters and send data without distinguishing between GET and POST methods.

Usage example:

```
$name = $_REQUEST['name']; // value of parameter "name" (GET or POST)
$age = $_REQUEST[age]; // value of parameter "age" (GET or POST)
```

It is important to note that using $_REQUEST may not be secure as it accepts data from both $_GET and $_POST. It is advisable to use $_GET or $_POST specifically based on the type of request expected, to ensure correct and safe handling of data.

$_SERVER:

- Contains information about the server environment and the HTTP request in progress.

- Provides details about the server, the client making the request, and other information related to the HTTP request.

- It is an associative array that contains several keys, such as:

    - $_SERVER['REQUEST_METHOD']: HTTP request method used (for example, GET, POST, etc.).

    - $_SERVER['HTTP_HOST']: Server host address.

    - $_SERVER['HTTP_USER_AGENT']: User Agent of the browser that made the request.

    - $_SERVER['REMOTE_ADDR']: IP address of the client that made the request.

Usage example:

```
$method = $_SERVER['REQUEST_METHOD']; // Request method (GET, POST, etc.)
$host = $_SERVER['HTTP_HOST']; // Server host address
$userAgent = $_SERVER['HTTP_USER_AGENT']; // Browser User Agent
$remoteAddr = $_SERVER['REMOTE_ADDR']; // IP address of the client
```

$_SERVER provides useful information to analyze and handle HTTP requests in a customized way, for example to verify the method used, obtain the client's IP address or manipulate the request header.

Both superglobals, $_REQUEST and $_SERVER, are available in PHP and can be used to access information and data related to the HTTP request and the server environment where the PHP script is executed.

Object Oriented Programming (OOP)

Introduction

Object-oriented programming (POO) is a programming paradigm that is based on the concept of "objects" and the interactions between them. Instead of writing code as a series of sequential statements, POO organizes code around objects that represent real-world entities or abstract concepts.

In the POO, an object is an instance of a "class", which defines the properties (variables) and behaviors (methods) of the object itself. Properties represent the state of the object, while methods represent the actions or operations the object can perform.

The POO is based on four main concepts:

- **Encapsulation**: It consists of encapsulating the properties and methods inside an object, so that they are accessible only through public interfaces defined by the class. This ensures controlled access to the data and protects the object from unwanted changes.

- **Inheritance**: Allows you to define a new class based on an existing class, inheriting its properties and methods. Inheritance allows you to create class hierarchies and reuse existing code, providing an organized structure and more efficient change management.

- **Polymorphism**: Allows an object to behave in different ways depending on the context. Multiple objects can respond to the same message (method call) in different ways. Polymorphism allows you to write more flexible and generic code, adaptable to different situations.

- **Abstraction**: It consists of abstracting the complex details and focusing only on the essential aspects of an object. Through abstraction, classes are defined that represent general concepts or abstract models, allowing for greater understanding and simplification of the system.

POO offers many benefits, including modularity, code reuse, ease of maintenance, and the ability to manage complex projects in a structured way. PHP fully supports object-oriented programming and offers specific tools and features for its implementation.

Classes and objects

A class is a model or structure that defines the properties and methods of an object. An object, on the other hand, is an instance of a specific class.

To define a class in PHP, we use the "class" keyword followed by the class name. Class properties, which represent the state of the object, are defined within the class using the keywords "public", "private", or "protected". Methods, which represent the object's behaviors, are defined as functions within the class.

Here is an example of class definition in PHP:

```
class Person {
    public $name;
```

```
    public $surname;

    public function sayHello() {
        echo "Hi, I'm " . $this->name . " " . $this->surname . "!";
    }
}
```

In the example above, we defined a class called "Person" with two public properties: "$name" and "$surname". The class also has a method called "sayHello()" which prints a greeting using the value of the properties.

To create an object of a class, we use the "new" operator followed by the class name and parentheses. We can then access the object's properties and methods using the "->" operator.

Here is an example of creating an object from the "Person" class and accessing its properties and methods:

```
$person = new Person();
$person->name = "John";
$person->surname = "Smith";
$person->sayHello(); // Press: "Hello, I'm John Smith!"
```

In the example above, we created an object "$person" from the class "Person". We assigned values to its "$name" and "$surname" properties and then called the "sayHello()" method on the object, which produced the desired output.

Classes and objects in PHP allow you to organize and structure your code in a modular and reusable way, making it easier to manage data and related behaviors in a single entity.

Builder and destroyer

Constructor and destructor are special methods defined within a class for initializing and freeing the resources of an object.

The constructor is a method called automatically when creating a new object from the class. It is useful for initializing variables, setting the initial state of the object, or performing other operations required to start the object. The constructor has the special name __construct() and returns no value. Here is an example:

```
class Person {
    public $name;
    public $surname;

    public function __construct($name, $surname) {
        $this->name = $name;
        $this->surname = $surname;
    }

    public function sayHello() {
```

```
      echo "Hi, I'm " . $this->name . " " . $this->surname. "!";
   }
}

$person = new Person("John", "Smith");
$person->sayHello(); // Press: "Hello, I'm John Smith!"
```

In the example above, we defined the __construct() constructor in the "Person" class. It takes two arguments, $name and $surname, which are used to initialize the class properties. When we create a new "Person" object passing the desired values for the first and last name, the constructor is automatically called and initializes the properties.

The destructor is another special method called automatically when an object is destroyed, such as when it goes out of scope or when it is manually deleted. The destructor has the special name __destruct() and can be used to free resources or perform other cleanup operations before the object is destroyed. Here is an example:

```
class Person {
   public function __destruct() {
      echo "Person object destroyed.";
   }
}

$person = new Person();
unset($person); // Manually destroy the object
// Prints: "Person object destroyed."
```

In the example above, we defined the __destruct() destructor in the "Person" class. When we call unset($person) to manually destruct the object, the destructor is called automatically and displays a message.

The constructor and destructor are useful for ensuring that an object is initialized correctly and that resources are freed up when they are no longer needed.

Inheritance

Inheritance is a fundamental concept of object-oriented programming (POO) that allows a class to inherit properties and methods from an existing parent class. It is a mechanism that allows you to create hierarchies of classes, allowing for code reuse and functionality extension.

In POO, a parent class is also called a base class or superclass, while a class that inherits from it is called a child class or subclass. The child class inherits all the public or protected properties and methods of the parent class, allowing you to use them as if they were defined directly in the child class itself.

To implement inheritance in PHP, we use the extends keyword followed by the parent class name. The syntax is as follows:

```
class Child extends Parent {
```

```
    // Definitions of additional properties and methods
}
```

Child classes can only extend a parent class, but the parent class can itself be a child class of another class, thus creating an inheritance chain or more complex hierarchy.

Child classes can access inherited members of the parent class, using the accessor operator-> as if they were members directly defined in the child class. If a child class defines a property or method with the same name as one inherited from the parent class, an override occurs and the child class version is used instead of that of the parent class.

Inheritance allows you to organize your code in a more structured and modular way, reducing code duplication and improving maintainability. It also allows you to add specific functionality or change the behavior of a parent class without having to directly change the parent class itself.

Let's see a practical example to better explain how it works.

```
class Animal {
    public $name;

    public function walk() {
        echo $this->name . " is walking.";
    }
}

class Dog extends Animal {
    public function bark() {
        echo $this->name . " is barking.";
    }
}

$dog = new Dog();
$dog->name = "Cody";
$dog->walk(); // Print: "Cody is walking."
$dog->bark(); // Prints: "Cody is barking."
```

In the example above, we have a parent class called "Animal" with a property $name and a method walk(). The child class "Dog" extends the class "Animal" using the extends keyword. The "Dog" class also has an additional method bark().

When we create an object of the "Dog" class, we can access both the methods inherited from the "Animal" class (walk()) and the specific methods of the "Dog" class (bark()). The $dog object will have access to all properties and methods defined in the parent class.
However, if we create an object of the "Animal" class, it would not have access to the methods of the "Dog" class.

Visibility of properties and methods

As mentioned earlier, the visibility of properties and methods within a class can be managed using three access modifiers: public, protected, and private. These modifiers determine how properties and methods can be accessed and used both within the class itself and by external classes.

Here is an explanation of each access modifier:

public: Public properties and methods are accessible from anywhere in the code, both inside the class and outside it. They can be used and modified freely. Usually, public methods are used as a public interface of the class to interact with objects.

```
class MyClass {
   public $publicProperty;

   public function publicMethod() {
      // Method logic
   }
}

$object = new MyClass();
$object->publicProperty = "Value";
$object->publicMethod();
```

protected: Protected properties and methods can only be accessed by the class itself and its child classes. They cannot be used or modified directly by outside classes. This access modifier is often used to define internal behaviors or functionality common to different classes within a hierarchy.

```
class MyClass {
   protected $protectedProperty;

   protected function protectedMethod() {
      // Method logic
   }
}

class ChildClass extends MyClass {
   public function methodChildClass() {
      $this->protectedProperty = "Value"; // Access allowed in a child class
      $this->protectedMethod(); // Access allowed in a child class
   }
}
```

private: Private properties and methods are accessible only within the class itself. They cannot be accessed or used by external classes or by their child classes. This access modifier is often used to hide internal implementations or sensitive data of the class.

```
class MyClass {
  private $privateProperty;

  private function privateMethod() {
    // Method logic
  }
}

$object = new MyClass();
$object->privateProperty = "Value"; // Error! Access not allowed
$object->privateMethod(); // Error! Access not allowed
```

The choice of access modifier depends on the encapsulation level and visibility desired for the properties and methods of a class. It is a good practice to limit access only to what is necessary to ensure the integrity and consistency of the code, avoiding direct access to properties and promoting interaction through public methods.

Proper use of access modifiers helps create well-structured classes, making your code easier to maintain, reusable, and understand.

Polymorphism

Polymorphism is a concept that allows objects of different classes to respond differently to a method invocation of the same name. Polymorphism allows you to write more flexible and modular code, as classes can be interchangeable without changing the general behavior of the code.

Polymorphism is based on inheritance and method overriding. When a child class inherits a method from the parent class, it can decide to redefine that method to suit its specific needs. This process is known as method overriding.

Here is an example of polymorphism in PHP:

```
class Shape {
  public function calculateArea() {
    return 0;
  }
}

class Rectangle extends Shape {
  private $width;
  private $height;

  public function __construct($width, $height) {
    $this->width = $width;
    $this->height = $height;
  }
```

```php
    public function calculateArea() {
        return $this->width * $this->height;
    }
}

class Circle extends Shape {
    private $radius;

    public function __construct($radius) {
        $this->radius = $radius;
    }

    public function calculateArea() {
        return pi() * pow($this->radius, 2);
    }
}

$rectangle = new Rectangle(5, 10);
$circle = new Circle(3);

echo $rectangle->calculateArea(); // Print: 50
echo $circle->calculateArea(); // Print: 28.274333882308
```

In the example above, we have a parent class called "Shape" with a calculateArea() method that returns an area of value 0 by default. The "Rectangle" and "Circle" child classes extend the "Shape" class and redefine the calculateArea() method to calculate the specific area of a rectangle and a circle, respectively.

When we call the calculateArea() method on an object of type "Rectangle" or "Circle", the behavior of the method will be specific to the class to which the object belongs. This is possible thanks to polymorphism, which allows objects to respond differently to the invocation of a method with the same name.

So, as we have seen, polymorphism allows us to write more generic and reusable code, as we can treat objects of different classes as objects of the same base class. For example, we can have an array of objects of different shapes and call the calculateArea() method on each object without worrying about the specific type of shape.

Static methods and properties

Static properties and methods belong to the class itself rather than to a specific instance of the class. This means they can be accessed and used without the need to create an instance of the class.

To define a method or a static property, we use the keyword **static** before the declaration. Here is an example:

```php
class MyClass {
    public static $staticProperty;

    public static function staticMethod() {
```

```
    // Method logic
  }
}
```

In the example above, we defined a static property called $staticProperty and a static method called staticMethod() inside the "MyClass" class. We can access these elements directly without having to instantiate the class.

To access a static property, we use the class name followed by the context resolution operator :: . To call a static method, we also use the class name followed by the context resolution operator :: and the method name.

Here is an example showing how to use static methods and properties:

```
class MyClass {
  public static $staticProperty = "Value";

  public static function staticMethod() {
    echo "This is a static method.";
  }
}

echo MyClass::$staticProperty; // Print: "Value"
MyClass::staticMethod(); // Print: "This is a static method."
```

In the example above, we accessed the static property $staticProperty using MyClass::$staticProperty without having to create an instance of the class. We also call the static method staticMethod() using MyClass::staticMethod().

Static properties and methods are shared by all instances of the class and can be used to store data or define functionality that is common to all instances. For example, a static property can be used to track a global value, while a static method can provide a generic utility or functionality that doesn't require an instance-specific state.

It is important to note that static methods cannot access non-static properties or non-static methods within the same class, as they are not associated with a specific instance of the class.

Plus

Include e require

In PHP, the "include" and "require" statements are used to include and import external files into a current PHP file. Both statements allow you to break up and organize your code into reusable modules.

The "include" statement includes a file and generates a warning if the file is not found or if errors occur during the include. For example:

```
include "file.php";
```

The "require" statement is similar to the "include" statement, but generates a fatal error if the file is not found or if errors occur during the include. For example:

```
require "file.php";
```

The main difference between "include" and "require" is error handling. With "include", if the file is not found or an error occurs, just a warning is raised and the PHP script continues to execute. With "require", however, if a problem occurs, a fatal error is raised and the script aborts.

You can use "include" and "require" to include PHP, HTML, text, or any other file type supported by the server. By including a file, the code inside that file will be executed as if it were directly present in the current file.

Here's an example of using "include" to include a PHP file:

```php
// file.php
<?php
    echo "This is the content of the included file.";
?>

// index.php
<?php
    include "file.php";
    echo "This is the contents of the main file.";
?>
```

Running "index.php" will include the "file.php" file and print both strings, producing the output:

```
This is the content of the included file.
This is the content of the main file.
```

Send an email

With PHP you can send emails using the **mail()** function. The basic syntax for sending an email is as follows:

```
$recipient = "recipient@example.com";
$subject = "Email subject";
$message = "Message body";

$headers = "From: sender@example.com\r\n";
$headers .= "Reply-To: sender@example.com\r\n";
$headers .= "MIME-Version: 1.0\r\n";
$headers .= "Content-Type: text/html; charset=utf-8\r\n";

// Send the email
mail($recipient, $subject, $message, $headers);
```

(Be sure to replace the $recipient, $subject, and $message values with your actual data.)

The $headers variable contains the email headers. In the example above, the "From" header is set to specify the sender's email address and the "Reply-To" header is set to specify the email address to reply to. The "MIME-Version" and "Content-Type" header specify the content type of the email (in this case, HTML text).

Note that sending email via mail() depends on your server configuration. Make sure the server is properly configured to send emails and that there are no restrictions or limitations in place. In some cases, you may need to use additional libraries or third-party services to send more complex emails or handle things like SMTP authentication.

Also, remember that sending emails may be subject to spam restrictions and spam policies from email providers.

Note: Using mail() to send simple emails may not provide all the advanced features, such as sending attachments or complex HTML. In these cases, you might want to consider using third-party libraries like PHPMailer or SwiftMailer, which offer more advanced and streamlined email sending capabilities.

Interact with MySql databases

To interact with a MySQL database using PHP, you can take advantage of the PDO or MySQLi extensions, which provide functionality for database connection, querying, and data manipulation.

Below is a basic example of how to interact with a MySQL database using the PDO extension.

Database connection:

```
$host = 'host_name';
$dbname = 'database_name';
$username = 'user_name';
$password = 'password';
```

```
try {
    $conn = new PDO("mysql:host=$host;dbname=$dbname", $username, $password);
    $conn->setAttribute(PDO::ATTR_ERRMODE, PDO::ERRMODE_EXCEPTION);
    echo "Database connection successful!";
} catch(PDOException $e) {
    echo "Error connecting to database: " . $e->getMessage();
}
```

Running a query:

```
$query = "SELECT * FROM table_name";
try {
    $stmt = $conn->query($query);
    $result = $stmt->fetchAll(PDO::FETCH_ASSOC);
    foreach ($result as $row) {
        echo $row['field1'] . " - " . $row['field2'] . "<br>";
    }
} catch(PDOException $e) {
    echo "Error in query: " . $e->getMessage();
}
```

Using parameters in queries (to avoid SQL injection vulnerabilities):

```
$id = 1;
$query = "SELECT * FROM table_name WHERE id = :id";
try {
    $stmt = $conn->prepare($query);
    $stmt->bindParam(':id', $id);
    $stmt->execute();
    $result = $stmt->fetch(PDO::FETCH_ASSOC);
    echo $result['field1'] . " - " . $result['field2'];
} catch(PDOException $e) {
    echo "Error in query: " . $e->getMessage();
}
```

Closing the database connection:

```
$conn = null;
```

Manipulate JSON

JSON (JavaScript Object Notation) is a human-readable, lightweight data format often used for transmitting structured data between a server and a client. It is based on JavaScript object syntax, but can be used with any programming language.

PHP offers several functions for manipulating JSON data. Here are some of the main things you can do with JSON in PHP:

JSON Decoding: To convert a JSON string into a PHP associative object or array, you can use the json_decode() function. For example:

```
$jsonString = '{"name": "John", "age": 30}';

$jsonObject = json_decode($jsonString);
echo $jsonObject->name; // Output: John

$jsonArray = json_decode($jsonString, true);
echo $jsonArray['age']; // Output: 30
```

JSON Encoding: To convert a PHP associative object or array into a JSON string, you can use the json_encode() function. For example:

```
$date = array('name' => 'John', 'age' => 30);
$jsonString = json_encode($data);
echo $jsonString; // Output: {"name":"John","age":30}
```

Reading a JSON file: To read data from a JSON file and convert it into an object or an array, you can use the file_get_contents() function to get the JSON string from the file and then use json_decode() to decode it. For example:

```
$jsonString = file_get_contents('data.json');
$data = json_decode($jsonString);
```

Writing a JSON file: To write data to a JSON file, you can use the file_put_contents() function in combination with json_encode(). For example:

```
$date = array('name' => 'John', 'age' => 30);
$jsonString = json_encode($data);
file_put_contents('data.json', $jsonString);
```

Manipulate JSON data: Once you've decoded the JSON into a PHP object or array, you can manipulate the data however you want. You can add, edit or delete elements and then encode them back into JSON using json_encode().

Manage files

In PHP, you can manipulate files using a variety of built-in functions. Here are some examples of the most common operations for manipulating files:

Reading files:
You can read the contents of a file using the file_get_contents() function. For example:

```
$content = file_get_contents('file.txt');
echo $content;
```

This code reads the contents of the "file.txt" file and saves it in the $content variable.

Writing files:
You can write data to a file using the file_put_contents() function. For example:

```
$data = "This is the text to write to the file.";
file_put_contents('file.txt', $data);
```

This code writes the string $data to the file "file.txt". If the file does not exist, it will be created. If it already exists, the previous content will be overwritten.

Adding data to files:
To add data to an existing file, you can use the file_put_contents() function in combination with the FILE_APPEND flag. For example:

```
$data = "This is the text to add to the file.";
file_put_contents('file.txt', $data, FILE_APPEND);
```

This code adds the string $data to the file "file.txt" without overwriting the existing content.

Reading line by line:
If you want to read a file line by line, you can use the fgets() function inside a loop. For example:

```
$handle = fopen('file.txt', 'r');
if ($handle) {
   while (($line = fgets($handle)) !== false) {
      echo $line;
   }
   fclose($handle);
}
```

This code opens the file "file.txt", reads the contents line by line and prints each line.

Deleting Files:
You can delete a file using the unlink() function. For example:

```
if (file_exists('file.txt')) {
    unlink('file.txt');
}
```

This code checks if the file "file.txt" exists and if so, deletes it.

Remember that, to perform read or write operations on files, you must have the appropriate access rights. Make sure you have the necessary permissions to read, write or delete files depending on your needs.

Password management

Password management is a key aspect of ensuring the security of web applications. Here are some best practices for managing passwords in PHP:

Use password hashing: Never store plaintext passwords in your database. Instead, it uses a hashing function like password_hash() to convert the password into a cryptographically secure hash string. For example:

```
$password = 'password123';
$hashedPassword = password_hash($password, PASSWORD_DEFAULT);
```

After that, save the hash string in your database. The password_hash() function will automatically generate a random salt for each password, which makes hashed passwords more secure.

What is a salt?
A salt is a unique random string generated and used during the password hashing process to increase password security. Its main goal is to prevent brute force attacks and attempts to crack passwords using precomputed hash tables, such as "rainbow tables".

Verify passwords with password_verify(): When a user tries to login, it verifies the provided password against the hash string stored in the database. You can use the password_verify() function for this. For example:

```
$password = 'password123';
$hashedPassword = '...'; // Retrieve the hash string from the database
if (password_verify($password, $hashedPassword)) {
    // Correct password
} else {
    // Password errata
}
```

The password_verify() function automatically checks if the supplied password matches the hash string securely.

Set strong password requirements: Encourage users to create strong passwords. You can set minimum requirements, such as a minimum length, uppercase and lowercase letters, numbers, and special characters. You can use functions like strlen() and regular expressions to check the requirements.

Use HTTPS for password transmission: Make sure you are using a secure HTTPS connection for the transmission of login data, including passwords. This will protect your information from interception by third parties.

Limit the number of login attempts: Implement a mechanism that limits the number of consecutive login attempts to prevent brute force attacks. For example, you can set a temporary block time after a certain number of failed attempts.

Keep databases secure: Protect your database from unauthorized access. Use proper authentication methods and enforce proper access permissions to prevent outside attacks.

Update Passwords Periodically: Encourage users to change their passwords regularly and provide them with an easy way to do so.

Avoid storing passwords in logs or log files: Make sure you never save plaintext passwords in logs or any other log files.

Outro

In conclusion, this basic PHP manual has provided an introductory but comprehensive overview of one of the most used programming languages in the context of web development.

We hope this manual has provided you with a solid foundation of knowledge to start developing dynamic and interactive web applications using PHP. However, remember that PHP is a rich and ever-evolving language, and there are many advanced aspects and features that can be explored further.

Keep experimenting and developing your PHP programming skills by consulting the official PHP documentation, participating in the developer community, and digging into specific topics based on your needs.

We wish you every success in your journey in the world of web development with PHP!